Football in America

GREAT MOMENTS IN
NFL HISTORY

Robert Cooper

DiscoverRoo
An Imprint of Pop!
popbooksonline.com

abdobooks.com

Published by Pop!, a division of ABDO, PO Box 398166, Minneapolis, Minnesota 55439. Copyright © 2020 by POP, LLC. International copyrights reserved in all countries. No part of this book may be reproduced in any form without written permission from the publisher. Pop!™ is a trademark and logo of POP, LLC.

Printed in the United States of America, North Mankato, Minnesota.

052019
092019

THIS BOOK CONTAINS
RECYCLED MATERIALS

Cover Photo: Gregory Payan/AP Images

Interior Photos: Gregory Payan/AP Images, 1, 6; G. Newman Lowrance/AP Images, 5; Anthony Behar/Sipa USA/AP Images, 7; Dave Clements/Sipa USA/AP Images, 8, 30; Darron Cummings/AP Images, 9; Arthur Anderson/AP Images, 11; Peter Read Miller/AP Images, 12–13; Al Messerschmidt/AP Images, 14, 15, 31; iStockphoto, 16 (top), 21, 26; AP Images, 16 (bottom); NFL Photos/AP Images, 17 (top), 27; Marco Ugargte/AP Images, 17 (bottom); Tony Tomsic/AP Images, 19, 20, 23; Harry Cabluck/AP Images, 22; Tom DiPace/AP Images, 25; John Gaps III/AP Images, 28–29

Editor: Nick Rebman
Series Designer: Jake Nordby

Library of Congress Control Number: 2018964847
Publisher's Cataloging-in-Publication Data

Names: Cooper, Robert, author.

Title: Great moments in NFL history / by Robert Cooper.

Description: Minneapolis, Minnesota : Pop!, 2020 | Series: Football in America | Includes online resources and index.

Identifiers: ISBN 9781532163753 (lib. bdg.) | ISBN 9781644940488 (pbk.) | ISBN 9781532165191 (ebook)

Subjects: LCSH: Football--Juvenile literature. | American football--Juvenile literature. | National Football League--Juvenile literature. | Football--United States--History--Juvenile literature.

Classification: DDC 796.33264--dc23

WELCOME TO
DiscoverRoo!

Pop open this book and you'll find QR codes loaded with information, so you can learn even more!

Scan this code* and others like it while you read, or visit the website below to make this book pop!

popbooksonline.com/moments-in-nfl-history

*Scanning QR codes requires a web-enabled smart device with a QR code reader app and a camera.

TABLE OF CONTENTS

CHAPTER 1
THE COMEBACK

In February 2017, the New England Patriots faced the Atlanta Falcons in the Super Bowl. The Falcons took a 28–3 lead in the third quarter. The Patriots looked like they were finished.

WATCH A VIDEO HERE!

Falcons running back Devonta Freeman leaps into the end zone for a touchdown.

Tom Brady attempts a pass as a Falcons defender tries to tackle him.

But Patriots quarterback Tom Brady didn't give up. He threw a touchdown pass near the end of the third quarter. In the fourth quarter, he threw another.

Then, with less than a minute left, the

Patriots scored a third touchdown. The

score was tied 28–28.

Patriots wide receiver Danny Amendola fights his way into the end zone.

James White (28) charges into the end zone to give New England the win.

The game went to **overtime**. Less than four minutes later, Patriots running back James White scored a touchdown.

The Patriots won! It was the greatest **comeback** in Super Bowl history.

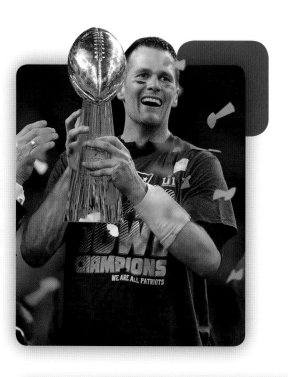

Tom Brady holds the Super Bowl trophy after leading his team to victory over the Falcons.

DID YOU KNOW? Tom Brady won his sixth Super Bowl in February 2019.

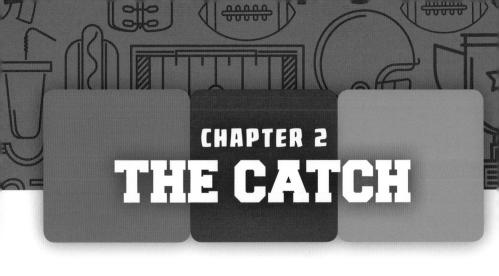

CHAPTER 2
THE CATCH

In January 1982, the Dallas Cowboys led the San Francisco 49ers 27–21. Only 58 seconds remained on the clock. The winner would play in the Super Bowl.

COMPLETE AN ACTIVITY HERE!

Joe Montana spent 14 seasons with the 49ers.

The 49ers needed to score a touchdown.

And they had just the guy to do it.

San Francisco quarterback Joe

Montana tossed a pass to the back of

the end zone. Tight end Dwight Clark

Dwight Clark spikes the ball after making the winning catch against the Cowboys.

leaped for the ball. He made an amazing

reception. It became one of the most

famous plays in NFL history.

Joe Montana (16) tosses the ball to 49ers running back Earl Cooper (49).

The 49ers went on to win the Super

Bowl that year. It was their first title.

And they weren't done. Montana led the

San Francisco 49ers to three more Super

Bowl wins.

Montana celebrates a touchdown against the Cincinnati Bengals in the Super Bowl.

DID YOU KNOW?

In January 1995, quarterback Steve Young led the 49ers to a fifth Super Bowl win.

TIMELINE

OCT. 3, 1920

The first NFL game is played.

DEC. 28, 1958

The Baltimore Colts beat the New York Giants in the first NFL Championship Game to go to overtime.

JAN. 14, 1973

The Miami Dolphins become the first team to finish the season undefeated.

FEB. 5, 2017

The Super Bowl goes to overtime for the first time.

OCT. 2, 2005

The Arizona Cardinals and San Francisco 49ers play the first regular-season game outside the United States in Mexico City.

CHAPTER 3
IMMACULATE RECEPTION

In December 1972, the Pittsburgh
Steelers and the Oakland Raiders were
in a tight playoff battle. Oakland led 7–6
with only 22 seconds left in the game.

LEARN MORE
HERE!

Raiders defender Willie Brown (24) tackles Steelers running back Franco Harris.

Terry Bradshaw led the Steelers to four
Super Bowl titles.

The Steelers faced fourth down on their own 40-yard line. Quarterback Terry Bradshaw heaved the ball. A Raiders defender closed in on the Steelers receiver. But neither player made the catch. Instead, the ball bounced into the air.

Franco Harris runs toward the end zone after making an amazing catch.

Steelers running back Franco Harris

grabbed the ball. Then he ran into the

end zone for a touchdown. It was one of

DID YOU KNOW? Fans called Harris's catch the **Immaculate Reception**.

the craziest plays of all time. And it helped the Steelers win their first playoff game.

A PERFECT SEASON

The Miami Dolphins had an amazing 1972 season. They beat the Steelers one week after the Immaculate Reception. Then they beat Washington in the Super Bowl. In fact, the Dolphins won every game they played that year. It was the first **undefeated** season in NFL history.

Miami Dolphins running back Mercury Morris tries to avoid a defender during the Super Bowl.

The Super Bowl in January 2000 was all about **defense**. The St. Louis Rams took on the Tennessee Titans. The Rams had one of the best **offenses** in history. But both teams had trouble scoring.

LEARN MORE HERE!

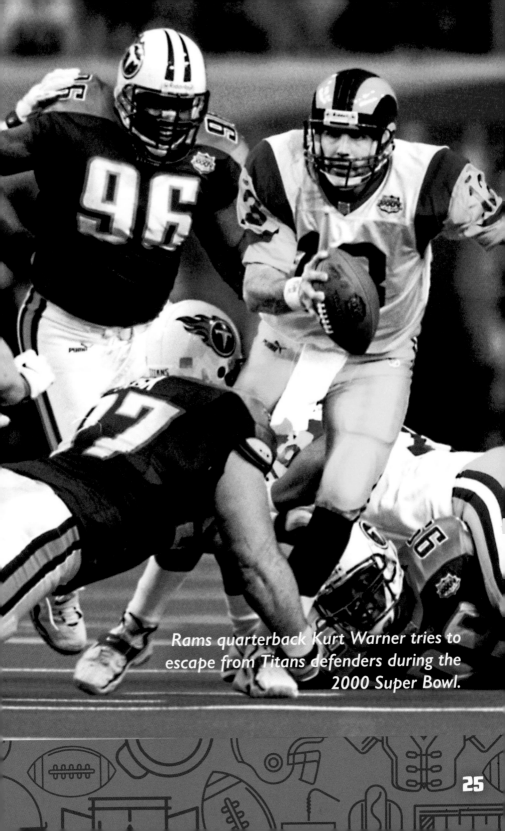

Rams quarterback Kurt Warner tries to escape from Titans defenders during the 2000 Super Bowl.

LONGEST PLAYS IN NFL HISTORY

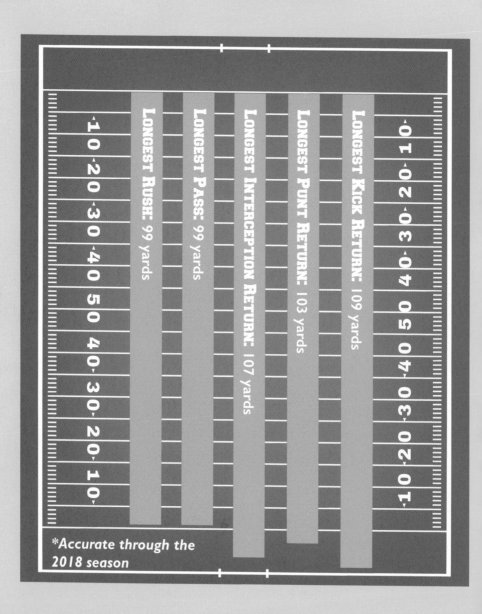

LONGEST KICK RETURN: 109 yards

LONGEST PUNT RETURN: 103 yards

LONGEST INTERCEPTION RETURN: 107 yards

LONGEST PASS: 99 yards

LONGEST RUSH: 99 yards

*Accurate through the 2018 season

With less than two minutes left in

the game, the Rams had a 23–16 lead.

The Titans needed a touchdown to force

overtime. They moved the ball to the

Rams' 10-yard line.

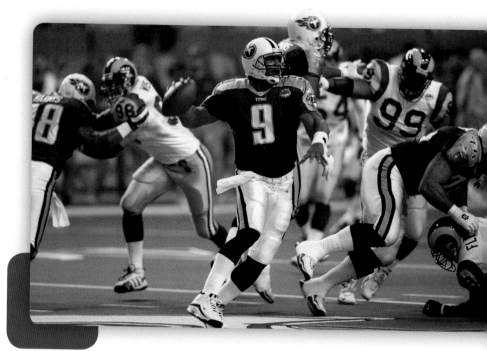

*Titans quarterback Steve McNair looks for
an open receiver during the Super Bowl.*

Only six seconds remained on the

clock. Titans receiver Kevin Dyson

caught a pass near the 4-yard line. But

a Rams defender tackled him before he

could score. Dyson fell one yard short

Titans receiver Kevin Dyson stretches for the end zone on the final play of the Super Bowl.

of the end zone. The Rams had won the

Super Bowl!

DID YOU KNOW? Rams stars Kurt Warner and Marshall Faulk both ended up in the Hall of Fame.

MAKING CONNECTIONS

TEXT-TO-SELF

Which of the NFL moments described in this book do you think is most impressive? Why?

TEXT-TO-TEXT

Have you read other books about athletes? How were those athletes similar to or different from the ones described in this book?

TEXT-TO-WORLD

Some great moments in NFL history took place several decades ago. Why do you think people enjoy telling stories about events that happened in the past?

GLOSSARY

comeback – a situation in which a team is losing but ends up winning.

defense – the group of players who try to stop the other team from scoring.

immaculate – perfect, without flaws.

offense – the group of players who try to score.

overtime – an extra period that happens when a game ends in a tie.

reception – a catch.

undefeated – having no losses.

INDEX

ONLINE RESOURCES
popbooksonline.com

Scan this code* and others like it while you read, or visit the website below to make this book pop!

popbooksonline.com/moments-in-nfl-history

*Scanning QR codes requires a web-enabled smart device with a QR code reader app and a camera.